Birthday Cards & Toasts
Express Yourself in Rhyme

Marcia Goldlist

CONTENTS

INTRODUCTION

Have you ever tried to write a birthday rhyme?
Did it take you a lot of time?
While here is a way that you can write a toast or a card
And it won't be hard.
You can write it for a girl or boy
And give them a lot of joy.
Or for a woman or a man
And they'll become your fan.
Take a poem which is complete
Or just use two lines for a tweet.
You can even take two lines at a time
From various poems and make up your own rhyme.
Or take out two lines at a time
It won't make a difference to the rhyme.
Try adding a few lines of your own
To set just the right tone.
You will make someone's birthday smile bright
By giving them your wishes which will be just right!

AGE SPECIFIC

Age 1

We hope that you are happy to be one!
And that you find life lots of fun!!
Your kisses and hugs we love to feel.
We all love you a great deal!

Age 2

A clown might be funny,
But you are our hunny bunny!
We are so excited that you are now two,
But most of all we want to tell you that we love you!

Age 3

It's hard to believe that you are already three
And learning your ABC's.
You are really very sweet
And being with you is a treat.

Age 4

Now that you're four
We want to see you more and more.
To be with you is so much fun,
That we don't want our time together to be done.

Age 5

You sure are special to me.
With you I love to be.
I love when together we play
Happy 5th birthday!

Bar/Bat Mitzvah

~Bar/Bat Mitzvah -1

With your skills we were impressed,
And it was nice to be counted among your guests.
May doing *mitzvot* bring you joy,
Much thoughtfulness may you employ.
We hope that you will always be a proud Jew,
And that being a good Jew is something that you will pursue.

~Bar/Bat Mitzvah -2

On becoming a *Bat Mitzvah we want to congratulate you.
From now on *mitzvot* are your responsibility to pursue.
For helping others your parents are both known,
But it is now up to you, for your life to set the tone.
We're sure that you will choose well,
And that you will excel.
May your choices be for the best
And may you always be blessed.

*Can substitute Bar.

20 Years Old

It is hard to believe that you are turning twenty,
On the other hand your accomplishments are already many.
You have already created your own path in life,
And you seemed to do it without any strife.
We are very proud of you,
And we wish you success in anything you decide to pursue.

22 Years Old

We want to wish you a very happy birthday,
With the hope that this year will be special in every way.
You are now twenty-two,
And we are not quite sure where the time flew.
May you be blessed with health,
And knowing that the most important thing in life is not wealth.

30 Years Old

Wow! You are now thirty,
And you still seem pretty sturdy.
May your love for *Bill grow,
And your discoveries flow.
May your health be good,
And you feel understood.
May you have a great year,
And your worries disappear.

*You can write the name of a spouse, or special friend, or something that the person likes to do.

40 Years Old

So, this year you turned the big four oh,
And we hope that to you this isn't a big blow.
Just keep enjoying your time with your kids and *your wife,
Because that's what is important in life.
Pamper yourself, 'cause that is key,
Make sure that for yourself some time is free.
May your work give you much satisfaction,
And with your co-workers may you enjoy the interaction!
We all wish you a successful year,
May it be one that brings you lots of cheer!

*For a wife you can write, "and as XXX's wife."

45 Years Old

Congratulations to our *man who is turning forty-five,
It is a wonder that with us you have survived!
This gift is just a little display,
Of our love for you on your birthday!

*Can be changed to gal.

50 Years Old

~50 Years Old -1

This year 50 you are turning,
And you realize that life is about more than just what you are earning.
Family is of prime importance to you,
And family get-togethers you do pursue.
We appreciate your caring
And all of your sharing.
Today we want to take the opportunity to thank you
For all that you do!
Here's a toast to you and your special day.
May this year be good to you in every way!

~50 Years Old -2

50 you are turning this year
And perhaps you approach this with a bit of fear.
Well, don't be worried
And don't feel hurried.
You're just reaching your prime,
And we hope that in health you will live a long time!
The hardest part of your work is done,
Now go out and have some fun!

55 Years Old

~55 Years Old -1

Congratulations on turning fifty-five,
And being very much alive!
I know that you don't really want to be reminded of your age,
But you've already done so much that by you we set our gauge.
May this year be filled with many things that get you to smile,
And many moments that you deem worthwhile.
We wish for you a healthy and satisfying year,
With good friends near.
Don't worry about the number of candles on your cake,
Or even any minor ache.
Remember that life is all about what you do when you are awake,
And we are sure that you will stay young with all that you partake!

~55 Years Old -2

Happy Birthday to you,
We hope that all year you never feel blue.
Now that you are fifty-five,
We hope that you will survive
Cause we don't know what we would do without you.
Our love for you is always true!

60 Years Old

~60 Years Old -1

So you are turning 60 years old!
It is a great age we are told.
If you don't want to do something just say, "Oy, I am so old",
Yet you are still young enough to have many adventures unfold.
You have 60 more years until you reach 120,
So good times and joy you can still have plenty.
We know that you have done many things of which you can be proud,
And that you are a great friend we will all declare out loud.
Make the best out of the rest of your life.
Try to keep a low level to your strife.
Enjoy your friends,
When the need arises make amends.
Wisely use your time,
Because all of it is prime.
It doesn't matter what your age,
Just to the fullest life engage.
To your warmth and friendship we can attest.
We wish you only the best.

~60 Years Old -2

Wow, you are turning six oh!
So, we really want you to know,
That we wish you all the best,
And you really do deserve a day of rest.
Half way to a hundred and twenty you are,
So as much as it seems bizarre,
You have only lived half your life so far.
So forget the salad bar,
Open a good bottle of wine,
And go out and dine.
Now you can reap the reward,
Of all that you slaved over on the drawing board.
Sixty is a great age,
From everything that we can gauge.
The hard work is done,
It is time for some fun!
Enjoy the second half of your life,
We hope that with it there will be minimum strife.
We wish you all the best,
And hope that the rest of your life will be blessed.

~60 Years Old -3

Everyone wants to wish you *"Congratulations" today
Because you have lived your life in an exemplary way.
So don't worry about the number of candles on your cake.
Remember that life is all about what you do when you are awake.
You have helped so many people in your life
(And you have a great wife.)
Now we would like to do something to honor you
So a donation to **the Food Bank we attended to.
We wish you good health and lots of reasons to smile
And many moments that are worthwhile.
May you have a year low in stress
And high in spiritual success!!

*Can write "Mazel Tov".
**Write name of charity.

~60 Years Old -4

So, this year you celebrate the big six oh
And upon your face we definitely see a special glow.
To celebrate you have decided to volunteer
Throughout the year.
This is just one more indication of how special you are,
And why in our books you are a real star.
You really deserve to feel fulfilled,
And to do many things that leave you thrilled.

65 Years Old

So you are now sixty-five,
And very much alive!!
We hope that you will have a great day,
And that your whole year will go well in every way!

70 Years Old

~70 Years Old -1

Seventy years old you are now,
And all we can say is WOW!
But really only one year older you have become,
So perhaps you need not feel so numb.
Another year of experiences and joys you have had,
So for all the extra good times in your life you should be glad.
And now, if you don't want to do something just say, "Oy, I am so old,"
Yet you are still young enough to have many adventures unfold.
Make the best out of the rest of your life.
Try to keep a low level to your strife.
May you be able to deal easily with any complication that arises,
And may you continually get good surprises.
May many things make you smile,
And not much make you hostile.
Enjoy your friends,
When the need arises make amends.
Wisely use your time,
Because all of it is prime.
May good adventures come your way,
And may you have at least a little fun every single day!
New experiences you should have plenty,
And blessings to count we hope you have many.
We hope that this year brings you many reasons to smile,
And that you do many special things that you find worthwhile.
It doesn't matter what your age,
Just to the fullest life engage.
We wish you all the best.
We hope that the rest of your life will be blessed.

~70 Years Old -2

I want to dedicate this to a special person who is turning seven oh.
There are some things that I really want you to know.
With you I really am impressed.
And I really do wish you the best.
You have not thought of life as a game.
You have always thought of what you wanted and taken aim.
You have really excelled.
High principles you have upheld.
You are really quite courageous.
To be your *daughter was rather advantageous.
Upon my life you have made a real impact.
Learning, travelling, always doing things in your life you have jam-packed.
Upon you maybe has snuck old age
But I know that you will tackle it with rage.
I hope that now you can reap the reward
Of all that you slaved over on the drawing board.
Seventy is a great age,
From everything that I can gauge.
The hard work is done.
It is time for some fun!
Enjoy the rest of your life.
May it be free of strife.
I wish you all the best.
I hope that the rest of your life will be blessed.

*You can change the relationship to friend, son, husband, wife, etc

74 Years Old

So you are turning seventy-four!
Well nobody can say that your life has been a bore.
You have seen so many places,
And put smiles on so many faces.
*We wish you another year of joy.
A special one with your first great grandchild who will be a special little girl
or boy.

*You can leave out the last two lines if they are not appropriate. Remember
that you can always take lines from other poems and add them on.

75 Years Old

~75 Years Old -1

You're turning 75,
And you just seem to thrive!
Whatever you're doing seems tried and true,
So continue what you like to do.
Good health we wish for you
And that a lot more happy memories you will accrue.

~75 Years Old -2

You have a heart of gold,
And you really don't act 75 years old!

77 Years Old

Seven is the number of perfection,
And we all look up to you with affection.
It's hard to believe that you're turning seventy-seven this year,
You keep up a busy pace and your calendar is never clear.
Best wishes for a very special year we pass on to you,
Hoping that this year brings lots of good memories for you to accrue.

80 Years Old

~80 Years Old -1

You have taught us to use our mind
So that in everything a good thing we can find.
So this year we get to take
A bigger piece of cake
Because we need more space
To hold enough candles to signify the years which you did embrace.

For us you always open your arms wide.
Security, love and advice you do provide.
We love just sitting by your side.
To be your *grandchildren we feel pride.

It is hard to believe that you are now eighty years old.
You sure don't fit into a mold.
You really use your time well.
At this game of life you are swell.
That you continue to be healthy is our hope
And that with whatever comes your way you continue to cope.

*Can be changed to relative, friend, son, daughter, cousin, children, etc.

~80 Years Old -2

So far you have lived 80 years long,
And we can see that you are still going strong!
Your body may not be quite as fast,
But a lot of wisdom you have amassed.
For your good health we pray
And that we love you we want to say.

90 Years Old

~90 Years Old -1

You are turning 90 years old
And you are still bold.
You say what you feel
And for help you still don't make an appeal.
Perhaps your body isn't what it once was,
But we can still hear your brain buzz.
Stay strong,
Keep moving along.
We are by your side
With pride.
Know that it is true
That we really do love you!

~90 Years Old -2

I have always been proud to be your *niece,
And as time goes on that pride does only increase.
In your lifetime you have really been influential.
You are one of those rare people who have lived up to their potential.
Your special deeds have been somewhat noted,
And upon you some recognition has been promoted.
Although respect you did not pursue,
It has been bestowed upon you.
You have been like a **father to me,
And advice you did give every time I did plea.
A ninetieth birthday is so special to share,
Especially with someone like you, about whom we all do very much care.

*If this is not for an aunt or uncle leave out the first two lines.
**Can be changed to mother, sister, brother or, "You have been a friend
to me".

98 Year's Old

It is amazing that you are turning ninety-eight
And you look so great!
You are so with it and it is easy to see,
That overall with life you are as happy as can be.

100 Years Old

As a child you must have laughed
That on the moon or mars could land any kind of spacecraft.
Yet here you are 100 years old
Having witnessed so many changes that did unfold.
Yet I can proclaim
That as far back as I can remember you looked the same.
You must have taken a potion
That keeps your brain in motion.
We are glad that we have this chance
To say that our lives you did enhance.
Many more healthy years we wish for you
And that more good memories you do accrue.
We hope that you know that it is true
That we really do love you!

102 Years Old

To my dear *grandmother who is turning 102,
We really do look up to you.
You have really used your time well on earth,
And given your life a lot of worth.
You taught **scrabble to me,
And our time together I always looked forward to with glee.
We often met for tea,
And your stories always charmed me.
Friends you have never lacked,
Simply because you were never afraid to make contact.
I want to take this opportunity to say,
That even thinking of you adds to my day.
May you continue to be healthy and cognizant of everything that goes on,
We really admire how you can go on so long without even a yawn.
You have shown that you do not take health for granted,
And to others this value you have also implanted.
I already can't wait until you turn 103,
For at that party I will also come and that is a guarantee.
And there is one other thing that I would like to say out loud,
And this is something of which I am very proud.
My life you really did touch,
And I love you very much.

*Feel free to change the relationship.
**Fill in something appropriate e.g. cooking, knitting, patience, cards, etc.

BELATED WISHES

~Belated -1

Okay *Bill, what can we say?
Your next birthday is already on the way!!!
But we really did and still do want to celebrate with you,
We so hope that over this delay you haven't been blue.

We are in awe of your early morning rising,
And we value your advising.
We all love coming in to your smiling face,
It is almost like a morning embrace.

We really value your attitude,
And hope for your kindnesses you feel our gratitude.
Of course we wish you good health for what's left of the year and beyond,
And that at least one of your wishes comes true with the wave of a wand.

We hope that this year brings you many reasons to smile,
And that you do many special things that you find worthwhile.
May you sleep well at night
Knowing that to us and many others you are a real delight!

*Write person's name.

~Belated -2

Your birthday is already past,
But that doesn't mean that for you our wishes have not amassed.
We wish for you a special year,
One of adventures and good times sitting around drinking beer.
Enjoy planning your life, your next meal and everything in-between.
The important thing is not to have everything a routine.
Remember adventure begins when work is done.
So take care to stay healthy but make sure to have fun!

~Belated -3

We want to wish you a very happy birthday,
And to celebrate with you even if there was a delay.
We hope that this will be a very special year for you
And that many adventures you will have time to pursue.
We truly wish you all the best,
In this coming year and generally in your life's quest!

~Belated -4

Though your birthday is finished,
Our wishes have not diminished.
*We wish for you a year of joy,
With lots of special moments with your little boy.
*Good luck with your new house,
We hope that you have many special times there with your spouse.
May this year bring you many things about which to smile,
And many activities which you feel are worthwhile.

*This rhyming couplet may be removed if it is not relevant.

~Belated -5

Even though your birthday was *two weeks ago,
We hope that you still feel that this **lunch in your honor is apropos.
After all it is only *two weeks late,
But we are hoping that with anticipation you did wait.
Truth be told we have been wishing you the best all along.
May you always feel in health and in soul to be strong!

*Write an amount of time or "a while".
**Can be changed to party, dinner, get-together, etc.

~Belated -6

Your birthday has come and gone,
But from our thoughts it has not been withdrawn.
May you spend time and resources on yourself,
Because if you don't you shouldn't expect it from any elf.
We hope that this year will bring with it many happy times,
And happy events which warrant rhymes.
Adventures we don't have to tell you to seek,
With this just continue with whatever is your technique.
We truly wish you all the best,
Keep living life with all your zest!

~Belated -7

*April seemed to sneak in,
And without me knowing it your birthday did begin.
I sure hope that it is not too late,
To wish you good things for your special date.
I wish you lots of happy times,
Even if for all of them you don't receive rhymes.
May you have lots of occasions which make you smile,
And lots of special experiences which are worthwhile.
May you be kept far from strife,
And may you feel satisfied with life.

*Write name of month.

~Belated -8

So *my dear friend your birthday has come and gone,
However, our wishes for you have not been withdrawn.
A lot of interesting trips we wish for you,
And that many new adventures you do accrue.
Health for you and your family is of course number one,
Without, it is hard to trek and have fun.
With a new grandchild on the way,
We hope that you will have much joy with the baby when **grandma you do
play.
We hope that this year will be full of just good things for you
And that lots of good memories you accrue!

*Put person's name or relationship (cousin, sister, etc.)
**Can be changed to grandpa, grandmother, grandfather, etc. Remember
that you can take out this and the corresponding line if they are not
appropriate.

BEST WISHES FROM FAR AWAY

~From Far Away -1

I value you and our friendship,
And enjoy our time when one of us visits on a trip.
I really enjoy conversing with you,
On the phone or by email when you are not in view.
I hope that for you this is a very special year,
Filled with lots of moments that you will always hold dear.
May you feel that you get lots of things done,
And be blessed with health, happiness and lots of fun

~From Far Away -2

We wish for you a very special day.
We are so sorry that from you we are far away,
But as you know people have to go their own way.

But just because we cannot be seen,
That we do not care is not what it does mean,
As to help you celebrate we truly are keen.

Good health we ask for you,
That many good wishes you do accrue,
And that your dreams you do pursue.

May you celebrate many more healthy years.
May you enjoy many good *wines with your peers,
And may you have many happy occasions to which your family appears.

*You may substitute anything that the person likes: books, movies, meals,
classes, etc.

~From Far Away -3

Your birthday has once again come around,
And I felt that I should say something profound.
However, all I could think of were wishes to bestow upon you,
And that to say thank you for all of your help was overdue.
All of us over here,
Are wishing you a very meaningful year.
Of course we wish for you good health,
And that you realize that of good points you have a wealth.
New experiences you should have plenty,
And blessings to count, we hope you have many.
May this year be a fulfilling one.
May you feel fortunate even before it is done.
Go and just plain have fun.
Remember that a brand new year has begun.
We are sorry that we are not celebrating with you.
In your honor we will eat a piece of cake and that will have to do.

~From Far Away -4

Once again it's your birthday,
And we're far away.
But we all wish you a healthy year,
And good wishes that are sincere.
You and all the family in health should be well,
And have lots of good things to tell.
One year older you have become,
And perhaps this makes you a little numb.
But really another year of experiences and joys you have had.
So for all the extra good times in your life you should be glad.
Of course we wish for you many more,
With your children and your grandchildren who we know you adore.
May you be able to deal easily with any complication that arises,
And may you continually get good surprises.
We hope that you do not have to do too many things that you loath.
Rather this year should be one of spiritual growth.
Of course we all wish you the best,
And all of the other birthday wishes with zest!
May good adventures come your way,
And may you have at least a little fun every single day!

SMS MESSAGE/TWITTER

~Message -1

Happy Birthday to you,
Many dreams this year may you pursue,
And much happiness may you accrue.

~Message -2

We want to wish you a happy birthday.
May good things come your way.
May you find much laughter
And may you live happily ever after!

~Message -3

No matter what you do tonight,
We hope that it will be to you a delight!

~Message -4

Cheers to you,
Many wishes we hope that you accrue.

~Message -5

We remember that it's your birthday today,
And we hope that you feel spoiled in at least some little way.

RHYMING COUPLETS OF 4 LINES

~4 Lines -1

This is just a little birthday token,
Hoping that our friendship is never broken.
May your year be full of nice surprises,
And may you be able to deal with anything that arises.

~4 Lines -2

We wish you a great year,
With lots of reason to cheer.
Be healthy, happy, and enjoy your gift.
We hope that it gives your life a little lift.

~4 Lines -3

We hope that your birthday is great,
And to it your whole family does relate.
Now that you are older and wiser,
To all of us you can be an advisor.

~4 Lines -4

Today is your birthday we're glad to say,
And we wish to celebrate with you in a small way,
Our birthday wishes will come at a later time,
But for now we hope that you will be happy with this little rhyme.

~4 Lines -5

With this I.O.U.
We hope that you will not be blue.
May this year be for you very fulfilling,
Doing lots of things that are thrilling!

~4 Lines -6

Happy Birthday to you,
We hope that a lot of good wishes you do accrue.
May you have a really good day,
And an excellent year that is terrific in every way.

~4 Lines -7

We wish you health and happiness on your birthday.
Celebrate with *Bill in a special way.
Be good to each other,
And enjoy being a mother!

*Write name of husband.

~4 Lines -8

There's more to a birthday than getting old.
It is also about on life getting a hold.
So over all that you have accomplished you should give a thought,
And we want to add that we all like you a lot.

RHYMING COUPLETS OF 6 LINES

~6 Lines -1

May you be blessed all year,
With an abundance of cheer!
May your problems be few,
And good times accrue!
May you have few trials,
But lots and lots of smiles!

~6 Lines -2

Happy Birthday – today is your day,
But then again, all year you seem to do things your way.
However we do want to proclaim
That we love you just the same.
But perhaps this year you could try,
To be not quite so much of a wise guy.

~6 Lines -3

We understand that today is your special day,
So good wishes we want to convey.
We hope that your whole year is sweet,
So as a token we have brought you a little treat.
We also want to thank you for all of the attention that you pay us,
We hope that besides our thanks our company is a plus!!!!!!!!

~6 Lines -4

You're whole family is together on your birthday,
So let's celebrate without delay!
Above all we wish you good health,
And we know that for you we better throw in a measure of wealth.
May you have an interesting fulfilling year,
Meeting lots of new people with whom you like going out to have a beer.

~6 Lines -5

Another year has passed,
And we know that a lot more recipes you have amassed.
We hope that this year you get to try some new exciting food,
And when you think about the recipes, us you do include.
But most of all we hope that you have a healthy fulfilling year,
One that has a lot of cheer!

~6 Lines -6

On a day which is sunny
We hope that you will use this money
To take your wife,
Which we hope is the love of your life,
Out for a meal
Which we hope will be ideal!

~6 Lines -7

So today is your birthday,
And in *two days you are going away.
It's hard to get a better gift,
As seeing **your grandchildren will be a real lift.
We wish you a special year,
Full of lots of cheer!

*You can change the amount of time.
**You can change this to seeing anybody specific or the name of a place.

~6 Lines -8

We wish for you to be healthy and strong,
Especially because we know that your days are very long.
May this year continue to bring you many happy times,
With lots of occasions to receive rhymes.
Continue to be relaxed with life,
Keeping far from you any strife.

~6 Lines -9

We hope that you are pleased with your birthday food dishes,
And more importantly that come true at least some of your birthday wishes.
We hope that health wise you will be well,
And that you live life to its fullest and not under a spell.
Finally we hope that no matter what comes your way,
You will remember that we are here for you every day.

~6 Lines -10

Happy birthday to you!
Soon in your arms you will hold someone new.
We wish for you an easy birth,
But no matter what we are sure you will feel the worth.
May you be well,
And everything just swell!

~6 Lines -11

We all hope that on your birthday you have a great day,
Getting a lot of attention and that the whole day is lively and gay.
We wish for you good health and lots of fun times,
And many special occasions deserving rhymes.
So – no procrastination –
Go and start your celebration!

~6 Lines -12

We hope for you and your family health for this year and beyond,
And that as a family you continue to bond.
Personally, may you feel satisfied with life,
And receive joy from your kids and your wife.
May good adventures come your way,
And may you have at least a little fun every single day!

~6 Lines -13

This is just a short birthday note,
So that you don't feel that strangled feeling in your throat
Thinking that we forgot and would let today slip away,
Without wishing you happy birthday in any way.
We hope that at least today you have been treated well,
Though we hope that your whole year will be swell.

RHYMING COUPLETS OF 8 LINES

~8 Lines -1

You are really a good friend,
And you help me with everything that I have to contend.
I always feel that to me you have an open door,
Because of you I can do ever so much more.
You are always there in the time of my need,
Without you I really could not succeed.
On your birthday I wish for you a special day
With a whole year of good things on the way!

~8 Lines -2

This is a special birthday and we are so glad that we are near,
Because in our hearts you are truly dear.
We wish good health for you,
And some adventures to pursue.
May you be surrounded by friends,
And enjoy good times by the tens.
May this be for you a great year,
Full of nothing but good cheer!

~8 Lines -3

It's your birthday today,
So we're going to tell you what we have to say.
That you're here again is a gift to us,
And we're glad you're not going away for a while in a plane or on a bus.
So today enjoy some cake,
And know that our wishes to you really are not fake.
We hope for you special things happen this year,
And you know that if you ever need anything we will be near.

~8 Lines -4

So, this weekend you have another celebration
To add to this year's elation.
Make sure that you take time for yourself once in a while,
So that you can keep your smile.
Keep an eye on all the good in your life,
To help keep away any feeling of strife.
We wish for you health and good cheer,
With lots of good things all year!

~8 Lines -5

So it's your birthday
And we just want to say:
We hope that you have a great year,
With lots of reasons to cheer.
In health may you be well,
And in general may your year be swell!
May it be a year low in stress,
And high in success!

~8 Lines -6

You are so terrific it is hard to believe,
So at least on your birthday accolades you should receive.
We love you a lot,
And although it may seem it your birthday was not forgot.
We're sorry that your gift is not on hand,
And we hope that you will be happy right now with our vocal band.
So we'll sing to you day and night,
Until we buy your gift and make it right.

~8 Lines -7

Happy birthday to you,
A lot of things for you this year will be new.
You will be going to a new school,
And we hope that to you the kids will be cool.
We value that you are a person that can be relied upon,
And wish you the strength for many adventures to embark on.
If you need us we will be there for a crutch.
We hope that you know that we all love you very much.

~8 Lines -8

To our dear *friend who everyone does revere,
We hope that you have many special moments this year.
Good health we are wishing for your family and you,
Although about your gift we are not going to give you any clue.
That you will enjoy your gift we have little doubt.
What it is we can't wait for you to find out.
In general enjoy your life as it is probably the only one that you will receive,
And good luck with what you want to achieve.

*You can fill in the person's name or relation.

~8 Lines -9

To a new apartment you are about to move,
And with this new location we hope your life does improve.
It certainly seems that your year is starting in a special way,
And we hope that your birthday will be a great day.
We hope that you have a healthy year,
And that every once in a while good surprises appear.
We can't wait to see you
And celebrate your birthday anew!

~8 Lines -10

It seems to us that you had a birthday last year too,
But that's okay as we like to celebrate with you.
May your garden bloom,
But too much of your time we hope that it does not consume.
May your garden always look its best,
And may it help you feel at rest.
We hope that for your birthday you get served some tasty dishes
And of course we wish you all of the traditional birthday wishes.

~8 Lines -11

Tomorrow is your big day,
And we hope that you do something special even if it is just to go to a café.
This year you have decided to shake up the status quo,
And in your life some changes you will undergo.
We hope that this year will be just great,
And that you will keep us up-to-date.
Your health should be the best,
And in anything you decide to do you should be blessed!

~8 Lines -12

So it's your birthday once again this year,
And we want you to know that our good wishes are very sincere.
We hope that you get to travel with *Jill to many interesting places,
And see many events which light up your faces.
Of course good health we wish for you both,
As well as spiritual growth.
That your goals you do achieve,
And that you always have something in which to believe.

*Fill in name of spouse, partner, your children, etc.

~8 Lines -13

It's your birthday today,
And we hope that you spend it in a special way.
Of course we hope that *Bill has something nice planned for you.
If not this is an issue that we will need to pursue.
We did miss talking in the morning with you,
But at least we hope that on a good breakfast you did chew.
Make sure that for yourself you do something,
And enjoy all the nice surprises that this day does bring.

*Fill in name of partner, or write your children, your family, etc.

~8 Lines -14

I hope that for you this will be a special day,
You really deserve much health and happiness without delay.
Of others you are always thoughtful and considerate and kind,
So I hope that on this day extra happiness you do find.
May your dreams come true for the good,
And may you feel understood.
May every day bring to you a special delight,
And may you know that you help make my life bright.

~8 Lines -15

Today is your birthday,
And there are some special things that we would like to say.
Like we wish you good health,
And to do the important things you have enough wealth.
We hope that you have a special day,
And that good things come your way.
Over you it is worth making a fuss.
Happy birthday from all of us!

~8 Lines -16

You have proven year after year,
That to high moral standards you adhere.
You always keep busy,
You almost make us dizzy.
May something special come your way,
Every single day.
May you never go astray.
May you know that for your health and happiness we do pray.

~8 Lines -17

It is your birthday.
But we are happy to say that you are not showing any decay.
For your birthday may your house be clean,
And your family treat you like a queen.
May all the hopes and wishes your family have for you,
Come true.
May your special day feel like a dance,
With everything going just right as you move in a trance.

RHYMING COUPLETS OF MORE THAN 8 LINES

~More Than 8 Lines -1

Some people would say,
That today is just like any other day.
But we know that birthdays
Are special in so many ways.
They are days on which we can reflect,
And think of those who have helped us with respect.
Yet we also look ahead,
With a special kind of hope that holds no dread.
Our birthdays may be known,
But there is something about them that is a private stepping stone.
May this year see you fulfill some of your dreams,
And set up new schemes.
Of course a birthday is also a time that good wishes others express,
So we wish you a healthy year, filled with good cheer, without any
stress.

~More Than 8 Lines -2

I think that a birthday is a good time to check and see
What we have accomplished and to what degree.
A birthday is a celebration of your life
Of the good deeds and accomplishments which are rife.
So don't worry about the number of candles on your cake.
Remember that life is all about what you do when you are awake!
You are always moving ahead,
So a birthday to you should not be dread,
But rather celebrated without fear
As you used your time well year after year.
See what new adventures will appear
And stay young for yet another year!
Wisely use your time,
Because all of it is prime.
It doesn't matter what your age,
Just to the fullest life engage.
We hope that this year brings you many reasons to smile,
And that you do many special things that you find worthwhile.
Of course we all wish you the best,
And all of the other birthday wishes with zest!
Go and just plain have fun!
Remember that a brand new year has begun.

~More Than 8 Lines -3

May you have much joy from your kids and your husband too.
Many good memories this year may you accrue.
With your life may you feel content,
And may you have someone willing to listen when you need to vent.
May you feel great meaning in your life,
And may you be kept away from strife.
May you have good health all year long.
May you feel physically and spiritually strong.
May this year be filled with many things that get you to smile,
And many moments that you deem worthwhile.
May you have a great year,
And may your worries disappear.
May it be a year low in stress,
And high in success!

~More Than 8 Lines -4

We're glad that today you are not away,
As we want to send you some wishes without delay!
We wish for you lots of days when your house stays clean,
And each of your children treats you as a queen.
May you find that as your children grow,
Upon you more and more respect they bestow.
May you enjoy many new dances,
And feel that in life you are making advances.
Just as you asked we are not making a big fuss,
But we are wishing you a happy birthday from all of us.

~More Than 8 Lines -5

So it is your birthday again.
We think that you had another though we can't remember when.
Perhaps it was about this time last year.
Well, we'll celebrate again so don't you fear.
You are certainly an important part of our team.
We hold you in very high esteem.
We love your way of finding out details,
And telling us all of the tales.
In person, or on the phone,
You find a connection that no one else would have known.
As you have a special way,
To get someone their family history to convey.
We listen carefully waiting for the twist and turn.
For these we really do yearn.
After each phone conversation you seem to have something to recall,
And with each story us you do enthrall.
But aside from your work and your stories, we want you to know,
That as a person our praise of you does overflow.
Important you make everybody feel.
The good in everyone you seem to reveal.
To others comfort you always bring,
So we hope that this year in your step there will be an extra spring.
To your fullest live your life,
Enjoy your children, grandchildren and being *Bill's wife.

*Fill in name of husband or write "and your wife" for a man.

~More Than 8 Lines -6

Today is your birthday,
And we hope that lots of good things are on your way!
Children who listen,
A house that does glisten.
Lots of happy times,
That don't cost too many dimes.
Good health,
And an understanding that the most important thing is not wealth.
May you always have someone in which to confide,
And good friends by your side.

~More Than 8 Lines -7

Happy birthday on this special day.
We know that you rather play,
But you are with us at work,
Your responsibilities you did not shirk.
We hope that you feel at peace
And that your joy in life does nothing but increase.
We hope you feel fulfillment in your life,
And that you don't have much strife.
We all wish you a healthy year,
And good wishes which are sincere.

~More Than 8 Lines -8

We wanted to buy something that would make you happy.
We certainly didn't want to get you something crappy.
So we thought perhaps we would get you something that would be
cozy and warm,
Even if outside there was a storm.
So we racked our brains.
In fact it felt like we were having labor pains.
And then the idea did come,
That a *cozy towel may help you cheerfully hum.
May you have a good year,
With lots of cheer!

*You can substitute something for the cozy towel

~More Than 8 Lines -9

We would like to celebrate with you your birthday,
And so we thought that from your *desk we could pull you away.
One year older you have become,
And perhaps this makes you a little numb.
But really another year of experiences and joys you have had,
So for all the extra good times in your life you should be glad.
Of course we wish for you many more,
With your husband, your children and your grandchildren who we
know you adore.
May you be able to deal easily with any complication that arises,
And may you continually get good surprises.
We hope that you do not have to do too many things that you loath
And that this year is one of spiritual growth!

*You can substitute house, books, computer, tennis, etc.

~More Than 8 Lines -10

You are generous in so many ways,
And your love of life is always ablaze!
You are satisfied with the little things in life,
Like looking at the stars, drinking wine and being to *Bill a wife.
Your smile is always aglow,
And in the morning we have to smile too when you say, "Hello."
Yet from serious subjects you do not shy away.
You are well informed and your opinions you know how to convey.
You add warmth to any room that you are in,
And certainly being your friend is for us a win.

*Fill in the husband's name, or for a man instead of "being to Bill a wife" write, "with your wife."

~More Than 8 Lines -11

Sometimes you're life is so busy,
That it kind of makes us dizzy.
So we thought of a gift,
That will help your gears shift.
We hope that after all of your running around,
It helps you wind down.
Don't forget to smile,
And take time to do what is really worthwhile.
May you feel that every day,
Something good has come your way!

~More Than 8 Lines -12

To you there is always a lot to say,
You are so giving and considerate and you wear a smile every day!
With people you really know how to talk,
And among nature you love to walk.
Your stories we love to hear,
Whether they are about your family, a stranger or how you went out
to drink beer.
There is no doubt that you know in importance health is number
one,
And that without a *vitamin, a day has not really begun.
So since you have your priorities set,
We would like you to know that your birthday we could never forget!
Our good wishes we want to pass on to you:
May good health and blessings meet you each day anew.
May you enjoy with your family many happy times,
And may there be many good reasons to write you rhymes!

* Fill in something appropriate like coffee, sandwich, kiss and hug,
newspaper, etc.

~More Than 8 Lines -13

You can always make us smile,
Because in any situation you can find something worthwhile.
Why something happened you understood,
And lunch is always really good.
Thank you for your positive vibrations,
They help us in life with our evaluations.
We hope for you that your wishes come out for the best,
And that this year you progress in your life's quest.
May you feel in body and mind to be whole,
And that over your life you are at least mainly in control.

.

~More Than 8 Lines -14

You have a great smile,
Which takes you that extra mile.
You often give us food for thought,
And we love you a lot.
You are definitely unique
And demand attention when you speak.
You are full of lots of life
And when the time is right you will make a great wife.
May this year be for you great.
May you be able to handle everything that you want to put on your
plate.
May you be well and whole,
In body and soul!

~More Than 8 Lines -15

Your big day has arrived,
And of our birthday wishes we do not want you to be deprived.
This is sure to be a busy year,
With new grandchildren far and near.
We are sure that it will be a year full of smiles and lots of fun,
And hope that you will feel that you have gotten things done.
We wish good health for you,
And some adventures to pursue.
May you be surrounded by family and friends,
And enjoy good times by the tens.
May this be simply for you a great year,
Full of nothing but good cheer!

~More Than 8 Lines -16

This lunch is dedicated to you,
And one more birthday that you did now accrue.
But by no means think that anyone would mistake you for getting
old,
Because we all know that you still have much energy to unfold.
Of course we know that you like to spoil everyone,
Because, simply for you, it is fun.
So today we would like to spoil you just a bit,
And a few appreciative words to you we would like to transmit.
So thank you for *all the calories that we have gained due to the
pastries that you have made for us,
And informing us of all the great places around the country which
you find and feel are a plus.
**We like that you share with us your special roses,
And thank you for letting us smell them close to our noses.
But most of all we want you to know,
That we wish for you a year full of health and happiness and that
your fulfillment does grow.

*You can change this to anything appropriate e.g. for all the help that
you gave us.
**If not appropriate you can remove this line and the next.

~More Than 8 Lines -17

Don't worry about the number of candles on your cake,
Or even any minor ache.
Remember that life is all about what you do when you are awake!

May you have good health all year long.
May you feel physically and spiritually strong,
And may life go along like a song.

May you always have good friends to share your joy,
And many experiences to enjoy.

May this year be filled with many things that get you to smile,
And many moments that you deem worthwhile.

May you have a great year,
And your worries disappear.

May it be a year low in stress,
And high in success!

May this be simply for you a great year,
Full of nothing but good cheer!

~More Than 8 Lines -18

Time seems to have slipped away
And once again it is your birthday.
Live it up big time
While you're in your prime!
Play hard and work hard,
But make sure that your family you do not disregard.
Hope that events this year keep you smiling
And that good times you keep compiling.
May you be healthy and happy,
And may life not be crappy!!

~More Than 8 Lines -19

May this year bring to you simplicity in finding parking spots,
And lunches that will not leave you distraught.
We hope that the kids wake up every morning without a fuss,
And that the dog is taken out for a walk without this you having to
discuss.
May life get a bit simpler for you, in short,
And may you feel that we give you at least a little support.
We wish you a great year,
With lots of reason to cheer.
Be healthy, happy, and enjoy your gift,
We hope that it gives your life a little lift.

~More Than 8 Lines -20

We can see that you are truly trying,
To keep from crying.
For on the table you do not see a present,
And this is causing you torment.
We really don't want to make you sad.
Then we would feel very bad.
So here is the deal,
We really do want to give you something with appeal.
But also different we wanted it to be,
And we hope that in the end you will agree.
We hope that our gift will make you smile,
Because for this special birthday we wanted to go the extra mile.

~More Than 8 Lines -21

I'm not sure why we celebrate the day that we are born,
Perhaps it is to warn us that wasted time we are to mourn.
We are to use our time well
And it is a push to get us to excel.
But you always have something on your plate
For a birthday you don't even need to wait.
You are always moving ahead
So a birthday to you should not be dread
But rather celebrated without fear
As you used your time well year after year.
*You've been just about everywhere around the globe
And the food and the wine you did probe.
You are not one to just lie around
You have people to see and things to do around town.
There are **more movies and restaurants you want to review I'm
sure,
I think that for aging you have found the cure!

*Leave this and the corresponding line out if not appropriate.
**Can substitute other things that the person likes to do for example
"many more museums that you would like to see I'm sure" or " many
more golf courses you would like to visit I'm sure," etc.

~More Than 8 Lines -22

To *Bill who just turned **57 years old
We think that you know that life is about more than just gold,
That there are many wonders to behold.

We hope that when your life you do review,
You find a lot of good memories you did accrue,
And that in your spirituality you grew.

We want you to know that you have friends by your side,
And we hope that you feel in us you can confide,
Especially when you have important things to decide.

We wish you a healthy year,
Filled with all sorts of good cheer,
And much success in your career.

*Change to appropriate name.
**Can change to any number.

ABOUT THE AUTHOR

Marcia Goldlist was born in Toronto, Canada. She has a Masters of Education from the University of Toronto. In 2000 she moved to Israel with her husband and 4 daughters. She is currently the mother-in-law to three and happy grandmother to three adorable grandsons!

Marcia began by writing in rhyme for family events. She has written for special occasions such as the engagements and weddings of her daughters and the birth of a grandson when her rhymes were read in front of guests. At work Marcia started writing rhymes for staff birthdays, office memos, to disseminate information, to welcome new staff and to say goodbye to the old. As a result of this she was asked to write for other people's personal and family occasions.

The compliments and encouragement that Marcia received encouraged her to put her poetry into books so that others could also make special occasions fun and meaningful.

If you enjoyed this book you may also like Marcia's other books:
~Cards & Toasts For Almost All Occasions:
  Express Yourself in Rhyme
~Cards, Toasts & Notes For the Office:
  Express Yourself in Rhyme
~Enjoying Genesis: The Bible in Rhyme

Keep your eyes open for Marcia's upcoming book:
~Enjoying Exodus: The Bible in Rhyme

Visit Marcia's blog Enjoying the Bible Online for discussion points and projects related to the Bible. You can visit the blog at http://enjoyingthebible.wordpress.com.

www.ingramcontent.com/pod-product-compliance
Lightning Source LLC
Chambersburg PA
CBHW030525290526
45786CB00004B/1626